I0424468

A Course
In Peace
And Joy

A Course
In Peace
And Joy

Kash Singh

Copyright © 2010 by Kash Singh.

Library of Congress Control Number:		2010910918
ISBN:	Hardcover	978-1-4535-4514-0
	Softcover	978-1-4535-4513-3
	Ebook	978-1-4535-4515-7

All rights reserved. No part of this book may be reproduced or transmitted in any form or by any means, electronic or mechanical, including photocopying, recording, or by any information storage and retrieval system, without permission in writing from the copyright owner.

This book was printed in the United States of America.

To order additional copies of this book, contact:
Xlibris Corporation
1-888-795-4274
www.Xlibris.com
Orders@Xlibris.com
83975

Who will this book benefit?

All of you who think you are missing out on your daily share of PEACE AND JOY.

By changing the way you perceive the world and your *"self"*, you open up the avenues that allow peace and joy to flow in.

By reading this book and doing the things I propose, you will raise your vibration on PHYSICAL, MENTAL, EMOTIONAL AND SPIRITUAL levels.

Anyone from thirteen to a hundred and thirty will be greatly benefited, race, religion or ethnicity notwithstanding.

JUST DO IT!

A BRIEF MESSAGE
TO ALL WHO READ THIS BOOK

Wellcome to your new world in which you will find PEACE AND JOY. You will create it within yourself, then you will feel compelled and impelled to extend it outward. You will realize that it grows within you as you extend it to others. And you will be amazed at how little effort is involved. After all, the best things in life are free.

I suggest you go through the book slowly, doing one *"lesson"* at a time and allowing your subconscious (or unconscious) mind to register it. This way many of your subconscious programs will change from negative to positive. I am a Hypnotherapist. We use hypnosis to create an altered state of consciousness which makes it easier to affect internal programs. There are folks who have internal programs of sadness, despair, etc due to negative programming from the past which registered so strongly that it affects their daily lives negatively. We help them remove & discard these, then we install new programs of peace joy, etc.

Life on the planet is too short to be wasted in thoughts not commensurate with peace & joy. If you are not driving, close your eyes for a moment, breathe in deep, and *think* peace and joy. Keep doing this and before you know it, these emotions will flow into you of their own accord simply because your mind will be programmed for the better.

SEE WHAT I MEAN

LESSON ONE

Always think positively

Make a conscious effort to remove all negativity from the mind. The thoughts we hold in our minds do filter down into the subconscious. This is where creativity takes place. As soon as your sleep breaks each morning say "I will have a great day today, I am privileged to be on God's green earth and I will have a perfect, happy and harmonious day today. Nobody or nothing can deprive me of happiness today." Take a few deep breaths, hold for a couple of seconds then release the air as you repeat this idea in your mind. You may choose your own words or ideas. Just be sure to keep them positive and uplifting. Your subconscious mind will suck these thoughts in like a vacuum. It will process them and gradually turn them into real life experiences. Doesn't take too long either. You're on the road to a new and better you

BON VOYAGE,

I know its a teriffic journey because I have travelled it.

LESSON TWO

Become a Joy Addict

Invoke the spirit of joy that dwells in you.

Can you do this? Of course you can. Please don't be numb to the thrill of being alive and being human. After all, we are very fortunate to live at a time when so much advance is being made in the fields of technology, science, medicine, etc.

Why do we always tend to limit our range of emotional experience? Why not go beyond the normal? Addict yourself to emotional experiences that go way beyond normalcy. This is not impossible, neither is it unrealistic. Start today to train your mind in elevating to and feeling a joy so intense that it takes you far, far beyond normalcy.

Delight in your very humanity, let the joy juices in your brain flow freely. Feel joy only as a human can. Do it now, do it always. Addict yourself to joy.

LESSON THREE

Keep that smile going

Always meet & greet people with a warm, friendly smile. You'll make their day. And if they don't return your smile, don't let it bother you at all. A smile is never wasted. They say emotions follow behavior. Hence smiling, laughing, etc precede positive feelings in us. Your smile does good to you irrespective of whether or not it goes good to others. Believe it or not, when Mc Donalds started to do business in Russia they hired their employees based on their ability to smile. Thousands of them braved the weather and waited in line for hours to get interviewed for jobs slapping hamburgers, frying potato chips and working the cash register. Most of them were disqualified because of their inability to smile. This happened during the cold war era. What a somber nation they were.

The earth is abundant with living creatures. The ability to smile is man's unique gift. Use it! Abuse it!

Smile Smile Smile

AND MAKE OUR WORLD A HAPPIER PLACE.

LESSON FOUR

Avoid Arguments And Conflicts

If peace of mind is your goal, avoid unnecessary arguments and conflict. Besides, such actions often lead to worse things, such as relationships going sour, physical violence, etc

Decades ago, in Los Angeles, California a friend and I got into an argument about the quality of South African gold. He insisted (incorrectly of course, & being misinformed) that the quality was inferior. I stated that it was pretty darn good. Early in the argument I pretended to give in and let him rest in his blissful ignorance. I was born in South Africa and know the quality of its gold. But I had no intention of starting a precious metals exchange and really didn't care. Months down the line he happened to see a documentary on South Africa and learned the truth. He then asked why I had agreed with him when I knew he was wrong. I said, "we could have argued extensively, but to what end, neither of us own gold stocks. And besides it might have impacted our friendship negatively. I value our friendship a lot more than I do my ego or the value of all the gold and diamonds in the world." We're still friends to this day.

PLEASE DON'T ARGUE—unless your job requires it.

LESSON FIVE

Let love grow in you daily

Repeat throughout the day, "I feel love because that is what I am".

The thought will help obliterate many of your negative emotions. Feel love in your home, feel it in your car, and in the bus & the train. Feel love at your place of work too. Feel love for all humanity and all life always.

Love is so powerful that it can sink into the subconscious and squash the lesser emotions and transport you to levels you've never experienced before. Maybe you have, in which case you know just what I'm talking about.

Love truly transcends all. Many are the vistas open unto those who attain the mountain top. And you're well on your way there.

UNCONDITIONAL LOVE IS THE BEST KIND.

LESSON SIX

Do not be prejudiced against those who are different from you in any way.

Prejudice takes many forms: Racial or ethnic prejudice, prejudice against the disabled (sad but true), prejudice against the rich (for having too much and not caring enough about the poor), prejudice against fat people and prejudice against the prejudiced for being prejudiced against others.

The truth about the matter is that prejudice is bad and can cause irreparable psychological damage. Those of us who are seeking peace must make it our express duty to guard against this at all times. Now I know this is not easy because of the way we were all raised, our cultures and traditions, socioeconomic backgrounds, etc,. but we must work on it just as we strive toward any worthy goal. Working toward personal peace and joy, and living in harmony with those around us are certainly worthwhile goals.

Accept the truth that people are simply different from one another rather than being inferior or superior. Different in outward appearances, worldly achievements, occupations, etc

You should be well on your way to a life of peace and joy by now and I do hope you're doing only one lesson per day. Better to skip a day than to do more than one a day. I say this because some will be tempted to read through the entire program quickly, put it away and get nothing out of it in the end.

This course has a lot to do with thought reversal and in order to achieve this you must do it slowly and put it into practice.

LESSON SEVEN

Keep an eye on that brain, lest it becomes a runaway train.

The brain is an organ and an amazing one. Just don't let it do its own thing. In your waking hours, you must tell it what to think and how to think.

It does its own thing when you're asleep. We have no control over that, of course, and this has a lot to do with the activity of the subconscious mind.

Think positive, uplifting thoughts always. Our thoughts are things. They are creative.

Everything that technology has created for our use and enjoyment, started as a thought or idea in someone's mind. I'm talking about everything—

THE GOOD, THE BAD AND THE UGLY.

Let your thoughts be good and let your creations be for good only. We can create a better world—

FOR EVERYONE.

LESSON EIGHT

Weathering the challenges of life

Into every life some adversity must come; no two ways about this. I happen to be a senior citizen now and I can assure you that I have been to hell and back on more than one occasion.

We must actually expect the tempest to come and try to do our best to prepare for them whenever they do come. Always expect the best and prepare for the worst.

Decide what you'll grab and run if you ever have need leave your home hastily. Acquire the necessary insurance coverage in time. If you're concerned about leaving your family in poverty if something ever happens to you, take out a life insurance policy while you're still able to. Cost goes up as we age, because insurers are in business to make money.

After you're done with this course and as you move through life thinking and practicing and meditating, you will be better prepared to face the storms as they bear down upon you.

LESSON NINE

Don't be overcome by fear.

Some of us allow fear to become the driving force in our lives. What could be worse? Fear inhibits us or holds us back. The only way for us to make great advances and move ahead is by conquering this inhibiting force within ourselves.

It's all in the mind. What starts there can end there. Someone or other said, "The only thing we need fear is fear itself." Don't be afraid of making mistakes either. The person who claimed that he never made a mistake, never made anything at all.

Every great success story is filled failures, mistakes and hurdles along the way. The inventor Thomas Edison knew this more than anyone else. This man encountered failure upon failure upon failure. His persistence paid off in the end and made our world a million times better than it was before he showed up.

Do some research in advance to know what you're getting yourself into, then JUST DO IT! Remember that he who considers everything ends up doing nothing.

You must expect to make mistakes along the way.

You must expect challenges along the way.

You must expect failures, but action is still the key to success in any venture.

DON'T QUIT, PERSIST. Fear cannot overcome you because of what you're made of.

LESSON TEN

Free yourself from the worry habit.

Some people worry too much, some are even chronic. Worry, in and of itself, is useless. It stresses you out and makes you sick but it does little to improve things.

If you're worried about your health, stop worrying and do something about it. I'll talk about self healing later on.

If you're worried about your financial condition, solve the problem by talking to an expert on such matters. Personally, I don't advocate bankruptcy, but the law does allow it for those in financial distress.

If your problem is such that you think you'll end up with the worse possible outcome, accept it mentally for now, then consider your options from that point on. Now think about how you would start building up or continue on from that point. It's usually not as bad as you originally made it out to be. This should bring you some measure of relief and minimize the worry. Remember that the worse has not yet happened, and that there is still hope. Another thing to remember is that over 90% of the things that we constantly worry about never really happen. Where is the point in all the worry now?

LESSON ELEVEN

About physical well being.

It is hard to feel peace & joy when the body seems to be falling apart.

Eating well balanced meals is great. Unfortunately, the majority of us don't to it. Our hustle and bustle lifestyles place limitations upon us, or we simply don't care a whole lot about what we eat. The good thing is that many fast food joints now have healthy choices. Why not pick these as opposed to the other stuff. Vitamin supplements are great too. They really do help, especially if you take one that contains a wide range of vitamins and minerals. We need them for the various organs to stay healthy and function well. Keep in mind that our bodies can't manufacture vitamins. They must be ingested.

Regular exercise is extremely important too. If you don't care for the vigorous type, a nice walk daily will do you a lot of good.

If you smoke please, make a good faith effort to quit, if you truly want to stay healthy, that is.

What affects the body, affects the mind and vice-versa.

LESSON TWELVE

Making dreams come true.

Auto-suggestion and biofeedback are mental processes that at are constantly at work without us even being consciously aware that they're happening. The human mind does work in mysterious ways. Through these means our desires can be transformed into physical realities.

This is how it works: Constantly desiring something causes faith to blend with thought, which filters into the subconscious mind. Here the thought translates into its spiritual equivalent, which is then transmitted to Infinite Intelligence and only in this form can a response be induced.

The trick is to keep repeating your desires until the vibrations are picked up by the subconscious and processed by it. In time you will be guided to ways and means of acquiring the objects you desire. Put auto-suggestion into practice and see for yourself. If you think you are lacking in faith you may even be able induce this through auto-suggestion and biofeedback.

I want to add that negative as well as positive thoughts are capable of being picked up, processed and translated into physical realities. This is the reason why I brought up the importance of thinking positively in an earlier lesson.

Best results have been known to have resulted when the suggestions to the subconscious are made just prior to falling off to sleep at night—as well as when your sleep breaks in the morning.

LESSON THIRTEEN

Be careful not to let your ego get the better of you.

I say this to you once but twice to myself because we are all victims of our own egos.

In order to have peace, our egos must be humbled. Most of our thinking is ego based. It has an insatiable appetite for "getting" because this is one way in which it confirms itself. The ego likes conflict too, this is another way in which it confirms itself. We all know how those with oversized egos are selfish, often in conflict and always wanting to strike the first blow. You made your ego therefore you can exercise control over it. Now whether or not you can overcome it completely is another matter. For now I'd say let's not get too carried away it.

I'd like to state one more thing before closing this lesson: Its cool to desire for and to own things of value and beauty as long as we don't do it solely for the purpose of ego glorification.

All things considered, we do live in a materialistic world.

LESSON FOURTEEN

The feeling of oneness with all being

Every time you have the chance, close your eyes and erase all thought from the mind. Realize that you can't do this if your mind is too preoccupied and you don't have some measure of inner peace. So when the time is right for you, close your eyes, then feel your consciousness stretching out and away from you in all directions and making contact with all life everywhere. Inhale and exhale at the same time (consciously) and feel the emotion of love, not just love but DIVINE LOVE. This exercise shouldn't take more than a minute or two, but it will help in raising you to a level of peace, love and well being known only to a few.

We are connected to all life, whether we realize it consciously or not. Accepting this reality and meditating on it will bring peace and joy.

LESSON FIFTEEN

For those of us lacking in peace and joy simply because we're are not making enough money.

In order to make money we must have a plan of action. Decide how much money you want to make. Then decide what you're going to do in order to make that amount of money. This may involve switching jobs or going to school to train and qualify yourself to make that kind of money. Hopefully you're lucky enough to be in a country where student aid and loans are readily available.

Now start doing the things you need to do to make the amount of money you decided will be good for you. Keep a journal in which you record your progress each day. Be sure to stay with the course until you reach your financial goal.

Now you're truly on your way toward that goal. And be sure to go on desiring better things, and letting the mental process of auto-suggestion and bio-feedback help you. Also, keep on saying as you move on ahead, "I can succeed and I will succeed." This in itself is a very powerful suggestion, the subconscious will surely accept it and process it, and set you on the right track.

LESSON SIXTEEN

Be an optimist, not a pessimist

For those who don't know, an optimist looks at the bright side of things always expecting good results, while a pessimist does the opposite. The laws of auto-suggestion work for both, whether or not they're aware of it. The pessimist fills his mind with negatives such as fear, doubt, unbelief, hatred, etc. These negative thoughts will filter down into his subconscious and sooner or later they will get translated into their physical equivalents and bring him misery, and he'll probably blame the world for it.

The optimist fills his mind with positives, he desires good things for himself and those around him, his subconscious accepts all these positive thought vibrations, and sooner or later he is guided to ways and means of acquiring them.

No use desiring a fine mansion with maid or two, a cook and a nice red Ferrari, and then excepting them to be beamed down from heaven. It won't happen. You will be guided to the means of acquiring such things. It could be a new job or career or even the urge to buy a lottery ticket, who knows you might even end up marrying someone who could provide you with such things. The universe works in mysterious ways. Be open to it.

LESSON SEVENTEEN

Let me be still and accept my reality as an Eternal, Immortal, Universal and Infinite Being.

Do conscious breathing and repeat this idea to yourself every time you can today.

We're causing the mind become whole again by inducing it to tilt toward the higher self and away from the lower self which I will talk about later on. For now, let me say only that the higher self is aligned with spirit and the lower self with the ego. They're often in conflict.

LESSON EIGHTEEN

Be conscious of your breathing and repeat throughout this day:

I AM BEING PROSPERED IN ALL OF MY INTERESTS BY DAY AND BY NIGHT.

Understand that the vision that you glorify in your mind, the ideal that you enthrone—this you will build your life by.

THIS YOU WILL BECOME.

We have learned that setting goals and

WRITING THEM DOWN

is a magical process. The law of attraction will go to work for you.

Know that your reality is sourced from the inside out and that you are the creator of your reality and co-creator with the universe. Abundance is your natural state.

LESSON NINETEEN

Let me feel perfect peace this day because of what I am.

Follow the same procedure and repeat the idea all day long. It will not be too long before you realize the magic of auto-suggestion and bio-feedback. For now, just bear with me and prod along because you're striving toward a worthwhile goal.

Peace and joy are truly fine goals in this day and age when so many lack it and are willing to pay a hefty price in order to have it. Please don't be thinking that I'm talking about alimony and child support here.

LESSON TWENTY

I have the power to overcome all things because of what I am.

Repeat, repeat, repeat until it goes deep down and is accepted and processed. You do have the power to overcome all things.

What we're doing in this lesson is that we're strengthening our minds in preparation for the adversities and tragedies that sooner or later befall us all. Now I'm certain that many of you folks have already suffered through some, as I have. And, sometimes it seems that no amount of preparation can comfort us when they do hit us.

LESSON TWENTY ONE

Believe in Miracles

I believe in miracles. But I believe more in our need for them. I also believe that every person, irrespective of his or her religion, should have a talisman. (From Greek telesma = consecrated object). A talisman is supposed to bring good luck. It could be a crucifix on your necklace, a statue of Buddha, Mary, Krsna, a miniature bible or Koran. It could even be any object that has special significance for you, like a rock.

Touch your talisman any number of times during the day or night and visualize the thing you want most at that point in your life. The desire will slowly sink into the subconscious which works in conjunction with the mind & spirit to turn desires into reality. Be patient, persist & don't lose faith.

The talisman helps in the reinforcement process. Of course you can make your request without it, but you'll be amazed at how many people, including once childless women have attested to its benefits. Strange but true!!

LESSON TWENTY TWO

Infinite wisdom abides in me and guides me in all things always.

Repeating this today serves to affirm yet another universal truth. We just never learned how to tap the source sufficiently.

This lesson helps to open up our minds and gain access to something we're entitled to but have not taken advantage of in any meaningful way We have neglected it for so long, now the majority don't even know they have access to it. The finite brain and the five senses have been depended upon so heavily that, with the process of time we have come to believe this is all we have. We have paid a price for this neglect though, by way of stress, depression and the lack of true peace and joy, and in some cases, insanity. It is the aim of this course to undo much of this. Most lessons must be practiced and not just read though, if you are to get the most out of this book.

When you're done with the course, go back to the one lesson that appeals to you the most, read through it, then repeat that idea throughout that day. Go on following this practice into the future, until you feel waves of peace and joy flow through you spontaneously.

The course can help change ones life for the better by changing the mind for the better. Auto-suggestion works because it induces change deep inside where the subconscious dwells, and it is here that the mind of the infinite meets you.

LESSON TWENTY THREE

I fear nothing because of what I truly am.

Breathe in, breathe out and repeat this idea every time you do. By the way, this lesson is not intended to make you reckless and turn you into a daredevil in any way.

What we want here is to lay aside all unnecessary fears that would otherwise inhibit you and hold you back from becoming the best that you can be. Remember that earlier lesson in which it was stated that the only thing we need fear is fear itself. How true this is.

Don't even fear death, the body never dies because it never lives. Having no life in and of itself, it does not die, but merely ceases to seem to be.

LESSON TWENTY FOUR

Let the light shine in me and through me always.

You can opt to become a beacon of light unto the world or a means by which Universal Intelligence increases its influence in the world. No need to take on the priesthood or become overly pious, unless you choose to make this your calling. Being a warm, caring, loving and sharing person is sufficient. I'm sure you already know a few people like this. They really do make a difference in our world. It would sure be nice to have more of them around because they light up the lives of others and make the world a better place.

Join the club today. Membership is free. It doesn't matter which religion, nationality or ethnic background you belong to.

How difficult is it to smile, give compliments, exercise a little patience and tolerance.

JUST DO IT.

LESSON TWENTY FIVE

Let me feel perfect happiness this day because of what I am.

Again, repeat the idea all day long in conjunction with controlled breathing. You must let it sink in and become part of your make up. This I cannot stress too much.

The best way to feel happiness is to keep extending it to others.

LESSON TWENTY SIX

The power of forgiveness

A forgiving mind frees itself because forgiveness brings release. Things such as anger, hurt and the need to retaliate and cause further pain and suffering are all gone now.

I admit that it is not so easy to forgive immediately after you've been wronged. Our egos demand immediate retaliation, but if we're able to let go of the ego, exercise a little restraint, forgiveness will become easier; with the passage of time, of course. Forgiveness heals because it is divine.

You are able to forgive because divinity dwells within you.

LESSON TWENTY SEVEN

Mind Body Healing Technique

Until one becomes adept in such a technique it is recommended that you consult your healthcare professional in the event of illnesses.

When this technique is practiced in conjunction with the doctor's care it can do wonders for you because now the whole person (Body, mind & spirit) is being affected.

Sit down in a quiet room. Shut your eyes and remove all thought from your mind. Be conscious of your breathing as you visualize a bright white light shining on you from above. The light enters you via the head then slowly moves downward lighting each and every organ in the body. It has come especially to heal you of your ailment, from the source of all life and all healing. It is DIVINE, and so are YOU.

Practice this technique for several minutes. Repeat it at your convenience. Those who do, heal much faster than those who don't. They have fewer complications too.

If you make a habit of putting this technique to practice you will be able to ward off many illnesses, stay healthy and make fewer and fewer trips to the doctor. You become adept at anything by doing it.

As a Hypnotherapist I do healing work on my subjects after inducing trance. When hypnotherapy is used as an adjunct to their doctor's treatment, the results are truly amazing. It is not unusual for patients to heal in half the time it normally takes to recover from major surgery, and with far fewer complications.

It's LIKE "WOW".

LESSON TWENTY EIGHT

Perception is everything and everything is perception.

Let me see a different world. A world of peace,love and joy.

Repeating this idea constantly causes a change in our perception.

We have the power to change the world by changing our minds about.

No kidding.

LESSON TWENTY NINE

Let the spirit of love, peace, joy, kindness, gentleness and truth shine in and through me always.

Constantly repeating this can truly transform one's outlook and ones life because what you are doing is that you are installing a new and better program into the subconscious, which we have learned to be about 90% of your mind power Now you're more likely to harmonize with the world than to conflict with it, and less likely to lose your peace. Money can buy a lot of things, but it can't buy you peace of mind.

I live in the entertainment capital of the world—Los Angeles, where else. It shocking to see so many rich and famous people pop up on the TV screen with emotional problems they seek to drown in alcohol and other controlled substances. If you got money you can buy all the dope the world has to offer, but not the peace of mind and joy that these people long to have. Will they ever get hold of a self help book such as this? Who knows.

LESSON THIRTY

You See And Experience As You Believe

Quantum physics now proves that our physical world is comprised of wavelengths of energy that correspond directly to our thoughts. Together with the wisest of mystics, they share an understanding of the nature of reality and a belief that we are SOURCE, NOT SUBJECT, of our world. They can tell us how our thoughts not only influence but CREATE our experience. Nothing exists until it is observed. Not only do you create the way you look at things, *you create the things you look at.*

When you lay yourself down to sleep each night, visualize and imagine something you would like to have at this time in your life. Visualize as if you already have it and understand that the power to visualize and imagine something is the very same power that makes it real.

LESSON THIRTY ONE

"THY WILL BE DONE, THY WILL BE DONE, THY WILL BE DONE". We have learned that this is the most powerful form of prayer (or asking the universe for something). We also know that before falling asleep, the critical (analytical) mind goes into abeyance allowing your requests to penetrate the subconscious mind which can devise ways and means of reaching your goals. When you imagine, try to use all of your senses. Put emotion into it too. YOU WILL SUCCEED.

LESSON THIRTY TWO

Your Mind Has Creative Powers

Know that you are co-creator with the universe and that you are always creating, whether you realize it consciously or not. You cannot not create. Your thoughts and feelings are the tools with which you craft your world quite literally.

Understand that the law of attraction or what we call resonance manifestation, is the principle by which you attract into your life that which is in vibrational alignment with your consciousness; your thoughts, feelings, beliefs and attitudes, whether you are aware of it or not. And this is why the first step on the road to successfully manifesting your desires is to become conscious of those very thoughts and feelings that are creating your experiences.

Know that you are connected to and supported by an all-loving, intelligent universe. This knowledge can allow and engage co-creation where synchronicities and serendipities abound. The "how's" are magically taken care of and events in your life seamlessly woven into a tapestry of dreams come true.

Know that the power of attraction is the power of like attracts like and the means by which you magnetically materialize that which you focus upon and are in energetic . . . . alignment with.

Know that you are a miraculous manifesting machine creating your reality in every moment. This law is an absolute. It does not discriminate, it simply is. Beware: it can work for you or against you. To attract what you really want, align your heart & mind to the outcome of your desire. Align with positive thoughts and feelings that palpably resonate and act as a magnet to your very goals. Your imagination is a gateway to the possible and a bridge to your subconscious (unconscious) mind—an integral key to manifesting your desires. This mind does not know the difference between what is real and what is imagined. Remember to activate all of your senses (taste it, smell it, see it, feel it hear it). Involve your feelings and/or emotions as well. How you feel about what you imagine will determine whether you successfully attract it or not. Understand that feeling is the language that speaks to the divine matrix, or the universe. Gregg Braden said, "feel as though your goal is accomplished and your prayer already answered. He authored God Code.

LESSON THIRTY-THREE

About Seizing the Moment

You are alive this moment, now, today, so be happy, at peace and at ease now. Don't allow what may have happened to you in the past to spoil the present for you. You are not living in the past or the future. How you feel now depends on what you tell yourself now or the suggestions you make to yourself now. Tell yourself that you feel peace and joy now even if you do not! Because these suggestions, when repeated often enough will register in your subconscious AND CHANGE THE WAY YOU FEEL.

Far too many people cannot feel happy and at peace now because of the many negative programs in their subconscious. When they seek help from people like me, I hypnotize them, deepen the state to the requisite level, then help them remove the negatives that keep surfacing and affecting HOW they feel in the present, even though what bothers them happened in the past.

I can't hypnotize all you folks, but what I can do is teach you'll self hypnosis, after which you can talk to you subconscious about removing old outdated programs it contains, and installing new ones that will enable you to feel the daily peace and joy you deserve. You acquired this book, you're investing your time reading it. Why not get the most out of it.

Sit comfortably in a place where you won't be disturbed by anybody or anything. No TV no cell phone, no pets. Keep your hands to your sides or on your thighs, unfolded. Keep your feet flat on the floor, unfolded. Breathe deeply all the way into your abdomen and feel your entire body get more and more relaxed with each breath. Beginning with the feet allow the relaxation to gradually move to the top of your head as you breathe slowly and rhythmically. As this happens repeat silently "I am relaxed, I am relaxed." Now feel the relaxation move from the top of your head down to the feet and say "I am *calm and* relaxed, I am *calm and* relaxed" as you feel the relaxation go slowly down. Then you will say "I AM NOW IN A CALM AND RELAXED *HYPNOTIC STATE*" and "I WILL NOT FALL ASLEEP BUT REMAIN IN THIS STATE FOR AS LONG AS I CHOOSE TO". You will now suggest to the subconscious mind: "All negative events and suggestions from the past are not relevant to my life now. They have no meaning in my life now. I gain release from all of them now. They cannot affect me in the present in any way whatsoever." You may then visualize and imagine loading all those negatives into the gondola of a large hot air balloon and see them float away till they become a speck on the horizon, never ever to return. You will then say "I FEEL ONLY PEACE AND JOY NOW" saturate your mind with these, then awaken your self by counting 1 to 5. Say wide awake!!

WELL DONE FOLKS

You may self-hypnotize using this technique any time you choose and give yourself relevant suggestions. A student may suggest, "Each and every time I sit down to study, my concentration, retention and recall are perfect. I can focus on my work like a lazor. I am never distracted in any way whatsoever. I am successful, I am successful, I am successful."

No matter what you suggest to yourself, always keep it in the *present tense*.

LESSON THIRTY-FOUR

Let Go of the Past

I now understand the only important time is the present and that the future is only an extension of the present. I choose to rid my mind of all fear and negativity and let peace and joy into my life *now!!*

Have a wonderful life, full of peace and joy.

The Writer

www.ingramcontent.com/pod-product-compliance
Lightning Source LLC
Chambersburg PA
CBHW050348290526
45785CB00006B/2689